People of Importance

SIR ISAAC NEWTON:
Famous
English Scientist

Anne Marie Sullivan   Mauro Evangelista

Mason Crest

Who is this boy in the window, and what is he doing? He has wonders to show you, if you will let him—fantastical toys, lifelike models, even the secret behind a falling apple. . .

He is not a toy maker or magician, however. He is a scientist, one of the greatest scientists who ever lived. He is Sir Isaac Newton (at least he will be when he grows up). With his playthings, he unlocked the secrets of the universe and set scientists on the path they are still travelling today.

On Christmas morning in 1642, a boy named Isaac Newton was born on a farm in the south of England. His mother's name was Hannah. His father died before he was born. When Isaac was three, Hannah married another man and asked Isaac's grandmother to take care of him. Isaac missed his mother and thought that maybe she didn't love him anymore. He felt angry. Sometimes he even dreamed about killing his mother's new husband and burning their house to the ground. But nobody noticed Isaac's angry feelings.

Feeling like nobody cared, he began to spend most of his time alone in his room. He was very quiet, barely speaking to anyone. Almost the only noise he ever made was the banging of hammers and the rasping of saws. Too busy with their own lives to notice, his mother and grandmother didn't see that Isaac had a very special gift. His hands were very talented, making all sorts of wondrous things from wood. Not only could he make everyday, useful things like tables, chairs and bookcases, but he also made miniature carts and coaches that looked and worked just like the real things.

Listening to the racket this lonely boy made in his room, no one could guess that one day his gift would help him change the world.

Starting school didn't relieve Isaac's unhappiness. At seven years old, he was smaller than the other children, who were mean to him. He didn't like the same things they liked, and he stumbled over his schoolwork. His schoolmates laughed at him and bullied him, giving him the nickname "Stupid Newton."

Models

As a boy, Newton's favourite pastime was making wooden models. These were his toys.

Isaac pretended not to care. He spent his time watching the world around him. In nature, he found a better teacher than any he met in the classroom. "Stupid Newton" was learning things his schoolbooks didn't even mention.

Even though Isaac was quiet and pretended nothing bothered him, inside, his feelings were boiling over. One day he had had enough. It was much like every other day. One of his schoolmates was tormenting him and calling him names. But this time Isaac couldn't hold his embarrassment, pain and anger inside a moment longer. He exploded, punching and kicking the boy until he cried for mercy.

Maybe he taught that boy a lesson. But it was Isaac who learned the real lesson that day. He saw that he didn't have to let people bully him. He could fight back. And if he wanted people to stop calling him stupid, Isaac knew he would have to try harder in school.

"If I hadn't had that fight, I may never have been more than a carpenter," Isaac said many years later.

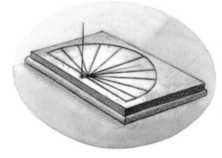

Sundial
This is the sundial Newton made when he was nine. Sundials tell the time from the the position of the sun.

When he was 12 years old, Isaac changed schools, going to King's School at Grantham. Grantham was some distance from his home, so he stayed with friends of his family who lived near the school. He was away from the farm where he was born for the first time in his life. The world suddenly seemed much bigger to Isaac. All the anger he had been holding inside poured out of him, exploding into passionate curiosity. "Why?" he asked, all day long. "Why do birds fly? Why do windmills turn?"

To answer his own endless questions, Isaac read everything he could, did experiments and built complicated models. To find out how windmills work, he built a model, copying a real windmill in the neighbourhood. It not only looked exactly like the real thing, it ground corn too.

As he watched his model windmill turn, Isaac began wondering about the power of the wind. How could he learn more about something he couldn't see, hold or measure. . . ? Of course! A kite! It was an everyday toy. He had played with kites himself. But now his mind looked at them in a new way. By flying a kite, he could measure the wind's strength and tell how fast it was going at different heights.

Kites had never been more fun. He made them in all sizes and shapes—round, square, diamond-shaped. . . He wanted to discover which one would fly the best. At night, he attached tiny lanterns to the kite tails so he could see them. His neighbours saw the lights in the sky too. They thought they were comets, which they thought were signs of bad luck. They were frightened.

Newton's name carved in wood
Like many young students do, Newton carved his name into a window at the school. This signature is held in the Royal Society.

Isaac's life was turning in a new direction. He was now one of the best students in his class. Then, when he was 15, his mother took him out of school so he could manage the family farm. Once again, Isaac was out of place. He cared more about science than farming, and his mind was always wandering. So were his pigs and sheep when he wasn't paying attention. They got loose, trampling his neighbours' fields and eating their crops. His mother found herself paying for her neighbours' ruined grain and vegetables more often than she liked.

One day, word spread through the neighbourhood that a big storm was coming. Everyone scrambled to bring the animals inside and save whatever crops they could from damage—everyone but Isaac. He also ran out into the raging winds. Ignoring animals and fields, he jumped this way and that, experimenting with the wind's force and direction.

First, Isaac jumped forward with the wind blowing on his back. Then he faced the wind and jumped into it. Of course he could jump further with the wind on his back. He and the wind were going in the same direction. Isaac measured how far he could jump each way. The difference told him how strong the wind was and in which direction it was blowing.

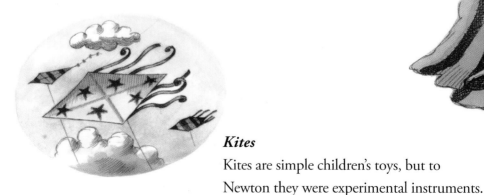

Kites

Kites are simple children's toys, but to Newton they were experimental instruments.

That did it for his mother. She decided it was be better to let her son be a great student than a terrible farmer. She allowed Isaac to return to King's School, where he worked harder than ever.

At school, Isaac found new, strange feelings inside himself. The man who owned the house where Isaac was staying had a stepdaughter about Isaac's age. They spent hours together making tiny furniture for her dollhouse. Isaac began to fall in love with her. But he was very shy. He still remembered the teasing and cruel laughter of his old schoolmates. He was afraid to tell this girl how he felt, so he never did. She was his first and only love. He never fell in love again and never married.

In 1661, Isaac was given an exciting new opportunity. He entered Cambridge University, a famous college with a huge library and some of the best teachers in the world. Going to Cambridge was like discovering the keys to a treasure chest brimming over with knowledge. It was a wonderful chance for a farmer's son, but he had to work hard for it. At that time, few people went to college. Most of the students at Cambridge came from very wealthy families. Isaac paid for his education by working as a servant. He served meals, ran errands and cleaned rooms for teachers and older students.

Studying and working as a servant at the same time made Issac's life very busy. He didn't care. He was so happy to be learning that he buried himself in

books whenever he could. He read everything he could find that was written by men like Descartes and Galileo, great scientists from the past. Isaac dreamed of following in their footsteps.

Even though he was spending so much time with his books, Isaac never stopped watching the world around him and wondering. He still asked, "Why?" at every step along the way. One day, as he was wandering the streets of Cambridge, he passed a piece of glass. A glint of light caught his eye. It turned out to be a prism, a piece of glass that casts tiny rainbows when light shines through it. His curiosity excited, he bought the prism and raced home with it.

After many experiments, Isaac understood that ordinary light, which looks colourless, or white, to us, is really made up of all the colours of the rainbow. The prism splits the light into stripes of violet, indigo, blue, green, yellow, orange and red. Since the beginning of time, people had been looking at rainbows, but no one knew where they came from. Light had been all around, everyday, from sunrise to sunset, but no one thought much about it. Then Isaac unlocked the secret, and other people began to wonder, "Why?" They asked themselves, "What am I really seeing?" Looking at light in a new way led to more discoveries.

Many of the things we use today would not exist if Isaac had not first asked, "Why?" Without Isaac's discovery, the world would still look fuzzy to people who need eyeglasses or contact lenses. There would be no powerful telescopes uncovering the mysteries of outer space. Scientists would not have microscopes to show them all those tiny things that human eyes can't see without help.

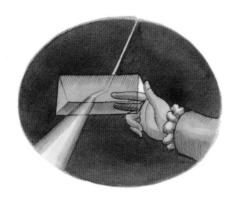

Prism

A prism is a three-sided glass instrument. When light strikes it, it makes rainbows.

Isaac graduated from Cambridge University in 1665. That same year the plague struck, and within days, thousands of people died, their bodies piling up in the streets. There were too few healthy people left to bury them all. It was a scary time, and Isaac knew he would be safer in the country. He had to go home.

Nights in the country were quiet. There were no bright city lights to dim the stars in the night sky. As Isaac gazed up at the velvety blackness, the bright stars seemed to call out new questions to him. For hundreds of years, scientists had been questioning the heavens. Now it was Isaac's turn. He wondered, why do the planets travel in circles? Do the moving planets affect the earth?

Even in the country, Isaac wanted to learn all that he could. One day he was sitting under an apple tree on the farm reading. Suddenly, a piece of fruit fell and hit him on the head. As he rubbed his head, questions began flooding his mind. The moon floats in the sky with nothing holding it in place, he thought. Why then does an apple fall to the ground?

All his studying and reading had taught Isaac a few things about the moon. Scientists had learned that the moon travels around the earth in circles. It acts as if it is attached to the earth by a string. But nobody understood why. Why doesn't the moon float away? Why do apples fall?

Isaac thought and thought. He did some math and thought some more. He realised that some force was making these things happen. He named the force gravity. While thinking so hard about that apple, Isaac made discoveries that scientists and mathematicians still use today.

The year was 1666. No one knew it at the time, but, thanks to Isaac, that year would change the course of history.

Isaac spent one full year in the country, staying until the plague was finally over. Then he returned to Cambridge and picked up his studies.

Apple
The apple will fall in just a second. It is about to become the most important apple in the history of science.

Isaac may have been quiet, but his brilliance spoke for itself. Two years after he returned to Cambridge, in 1669, the university made him a professor. He was the youngest mathematics professor ever to teach at Cambridge. He was only 26.

Sadly, Isaac could be hard for people to get along with because he was so shy and so afraid of being hurt. His classes were hard to understand for most people. Very few students came to hear him.

Although Isaac was not a very successful teacher, he was still a brilliant thinker. Using what he had learned about light, Isaac made a model telescope. At that time, telescopes were huge. Some of them were longer than half a football field. Isaac's was less than one foot long. Yet objects seen through those enormous old telescopes never looked so large and clear as they did through Isaac's tiny telescope.

In 1671, Isaac showed his telescope to the Royal Society, a group of scientists who shared their discoveries with each other. The scientists at the Royal Society were so excited by this new invention that they showed it to the king, Charles II. They invited Isaac to join the society and asked him to write a paper describing his telescope. Robert Hooke, a member of the Royal Society, was asked to present the paper.

Hooke argued with Isaac's discoveries, and Isaac found that he couldn't stand having his ideas criticised. Feeling hurt, Isaac decided not to share his ideas with people anymore.

Disagreeing with Robert Hooke turned Isaac away from mathematics and physics for many years. Instead, he began studying alchemy, the beginnings of chemistry. Then, 20 years later, a man named Halley convinced Isaac that he should write a book telling people his ideas about gravity.

Telescope
Isaac made every part of this telescope with his own hands. One look through the eyepiece will reveal distant planets and far-off galaxies.

Isaac spent two years writing this book. During this time, he barely rested or slept. When he was finished, he had completed three volumes. They were all published under one title, *Principia*.

In *Principia*, Isaac finally allowed the world to see all his ideas and theories. He described how objects move in space and also how two different objects moving in space affect each other. According to Isaac, all the objects in the universe are pulled, or attracted, toward each other. He showed that objects move the way they do because forces push them in a certain direction or move them at a certain speed.

Isaac taught his readers how to describe and understand these forces using math. This powerful new type of math is named calculus. To this day, scientists, engineers and businesspeople use calculus to solve problems and make new discoveries.

After *Principia* was published, scientists suddenly found they could use Isaac's ideas to predict what objects would do. They could use math problems to describe anything, from a rolling ball to an orbiting planet.

But how else are Isaac's ideas useful? Actually, people still use them every day to create things we use and take for granted. For instance, engineers have to understand the movement of a speeding car before they can design brakes that will stop it. Also, the forces that Isaac described hold up the long bridges that now stretch across rivers. Without understanding these forces, no one could be sure that these bridges would stay up once they were built. And it is very important to understand the movement of the planets before planning a rocket's flight.

Billiards
Have you ever seen a billiard table? Knowing Isaac's theories will help you move those balls into the pockets every time.

Before Isaac's discoveries, people's lives changed very little over hundreds of years. After his discoveries, people found that many things were possible—things they had only dreamed about in their imaginations. One invention followed another very quickly. Today, life changes more rapidly all the time. By constantly asking, "Why?" Isaac changed the world.

Principia stunned the world. When the first volume appeared, people began calling Isaac a genius. But Isaac's old enemy, Robert Hooke, came back to spoil his success again. Hooke claimed that Isaac stole ideas for *Principia* from an article he had written. Isaac was very angry. He had been holding all these ideas inside for 20 years. Besides, Hooke had never used math to prove his scientific theories.

All his life, Isaac had run away from his problems with people. When he felt he was being attacked, he hid inside himself. Now, he thought about giving up on the third volume of *Principia*. But this time, his anger wouldn't let him run away. Before long, the world saw that Hooke was lying. Mathematics backed up all Isaac's ideas. Hooke had no such proof. For Isaac, the truth won the battle.

In 1671, Isaac had backed away from the Royal Society. In 1703, the Royal Society elected Isaac Newton to be its chairman. Then, in 1705, Queen Anne made Isaac a knight. He could now be called Sir Isaac Newton, the first knight of scientific achievement.

After years of silence, Isaac's accomplishments were finally recognised.

But his battles were not over yet. Just as he had argued with Hooke, he later argued with a mathematician named Liebniz about who invented calculus. This time, he didn't run away. By now, he was a famous scientist. Isaac attacked his enemies with all the force he had.

Principia
Published in 1687, Newton's book stunned the world. People began calling Issac a genius.

Newton's curiosity was never satisfied. He saw the same things that everyone else saw. But unlike everyone else, he always needed to know "Why?" Unfortunately, Isaac was also driven by anger. Sometimes his anger felt like fire, so hot

it burned him and anyone who came near him. Getting along with other people was always Isaac's downfall.

Like all human beings, Isaac had his flaws. But his great accomplishments shine far brighter than his little mistakes. He died nearly 300 years ago. Yet today we rely all the time on technology that his ideas made possible. From television to space travel, humanity has been building on Isaac's discoveries ever since he first showed them to the world.

Isaac said, "If I saw farther than others, it was because I was standing on the shoulders of giants." He meant that he built his theories on the work of great scientists who lived before him. He needed to know what they had learned before he could add on to it. Since then, generations of scientists have been able to build on his work in the same way.

Standing on the shoulders of the giants of science, we can see farther and reach higher all the time. One scientific discovery building on another, we come closer and closer to understanding our universe and how it works.

DID YOU KNOW?

MAKING SUNDIALS

Isaac noticed that trees' shadows change all day long. He figured out that the shadows move along with the position of the sun as it appears to travel across the sky from east to west. He drove a nail through the centre of a round stone. Carving lines into the stone with a knife, he divided it into even sections, as if he were cutting a pie. The shadow of the nail moved around the circle during the day. From the position of the shadow, Isaac could tell the time of day.

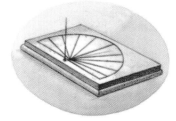

PLAYING WITH PRISMS

Isaac closed the shutters and curtains to his room. He left it completely dark except for one tiny point of sunlight that shone through a small hole in one of the shutters. He held his prism up to this point of light. After passing through the prism, the beam of light reappeared as a rainbow.

Isaac wondered whether the colours came from the glass of the prism or from the beam of light. To find out, he covered all the bands of the rainbow except for the red one. He let this red light shine through another prism. Instead of casting a rainbow this time, the prism cast only red light on the wall. He tried again with all the different colours of the rainbow. Each time, the only colour that appeared on the wall was the colour Isaac shone through the prism. Finally, he let the entire rainbow shine through the second prism at one time—and white light appeared.

So the colours came from the light, not from the glass. White light is made from a combination of seven different colours. To prove this idea, Isaac made a spinning top out of cardboard. He painted it like a rainbow. When he spun the top, all the colours disappeared, and it looked white.

THE EARTH'S GRAVITY

Isaac was convinced that the earth had pulled the apple to the ground. He also believed that the same force that pulled on the apple was pulling on the moon to hold it in its orbit around the earth. But why did the apple fall to the ground while the moon stayed in place hundreds of thousands of miles away?

As a child, he had played a game with a stone tied to a string. The stone was whirled around in circles in the air. If he thought of his hand as the earth and the stone as the moon, then the string was the invisible force holding them together.

He decided that the same type of invisible force must hold all the bodies in the universe together. That is why the planets revolve around the sun, and the moons revolve around the planets. In fact, everything in the universe is attracted to every other thing. So the movement of one object affects the movement of all objects.

THE TELESCOPE

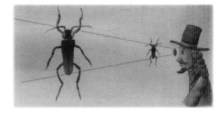

In Isaac's day, refracting telescopes were as long as 200 feet. The lens inside these telescopes made objects look blurry and full of rainbows. So Isaac used a mirror instead of a lens in his telescope. A mirror would reflect the light without breaking it into a rainbow. When light hits the surface of a mirror, it bounces off and changes direction, but the light itself remains the same. It works much like a rubber ball hitting a wall. It bounces and changes direction, but the shape of the ball does not change.

The reflected light hits the eye at an angle, and the image is made larger, with no rainbows or blurring. This type of telescope is called a reflecting telescope. Reflecting telescopes do not have to be longer to make objects look bigger, so Isaac's telescope was much easier to use than the awkward refracting telescope.

NEWTON'S LAWS

THE FIRST LAW

Every object will either remain at rest or stay in motion in a straight line unless a force acts on it to change its state. This idea is known as inertia.

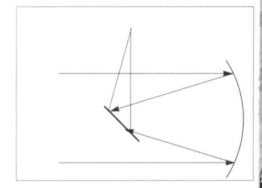

THE SECOND LAW

How much an object's motion will change is directly related to the amount of force applied to it. The motion will change in the direction of the straight line at which the force is applied.

THE THIRD LAW

To every action there is an equal and opposite reaction.

BIOGRAPHY

Author Anne Marie Sullivan received a degree in English from Temple University. She has worked in the publishing field as a writer and editor. She lives with her husband and three children in the Philadelphia suburbs.

Mason Crest
450 Parkway Drive, Suite D
Broomall, PA 19008
www.masoncrest.com

Printed and bound in the United States of America.

First printing
9 8 7 6 5 4 3 2 1

Series ISBN: 978-1-4222-2839-5
ISBN: 978-1-4222-2856-2
ebook ISBN: 978-1-4222-8976-1

Cataloging-in-Publication Data on file with the Library of Congress.

Produced by Vestal Creative Services.
www.vestalcreative.com
Illustrations copyright © 1998 Mauro Evangelista.